T0132234

It's All About
THE CHILDCARE

Maria Sadler
Illustrated by Maria Sadler and Wee Friends

WestBow Press books may be ordered through booksellers or by contacting:

WestBow Press
A Division of Thomas Nelson & Zondervan
1663 Liberty Drive
Bloomington, IN 47403
www.westbowpress.com
1 (866) 928-1240

Because of the dynamic nature of the Internet, any web addresses or links contained in this book may have changed since publication and may no longer be valid. The views expressed in this work are solely those of the author and do not necessarily reflect the views of the publisher, and the publisher hereby disclaims any responsibility for them.

Scriptures taken from the Holy Bible, New International Version®, NIV®. Copyright © 1973, 1978, 1984, 2011 by Biblica, Inc.™ Used by permission of Zondervan. All rights reserved worldwide. www.zondervan.com The "NIV" and "New International Version" are trademarks registered in the United States Patent and Trademark Office by Biblica, Inc.

Any people depicted in stock imagery provided by Getty Images are models, and such images are being used for illustrative purposes only. Certain stock imagery © Getty Images.

ISBN: 978-1-9736-4660-0 (sc)
ISBN: 978-1-9736-4661-7 (e)

Library of Congress Control Number: 2018913982

Print information available on the last page.

WestBow Press rev. date: 01/30/2019

WestBow
PRESS®
A DIVISION OF THOMAS NELSON
& ZONDERVAN

I dedicate this book to my Heavenly Father. Thank You for Your faithfulness and guidance every step of the way. Thank You for my family whom I love very much. And thank all of you whom the Lord has used over the years to help me complete this book. You know who you are. I couldn't have done it without you.

Thank You
Heavenly Father

John 15:5... I am the vine. You are the branches...
Apart from Me you can do nothing.

Chapter 1

What Do You Want
To Do? Let's........

B, b

Let's have story time with Bonnie Bucket.

D, d

Let's dance! It's music movement time!

L, l

Let's play ball.

T, t

Let's play trains.
Choo-Choo!

U, u

Let's play with my umbrella outside in the rain.

Let's write our
ABC's.

Let's draw pictures.

Let's play dress up.

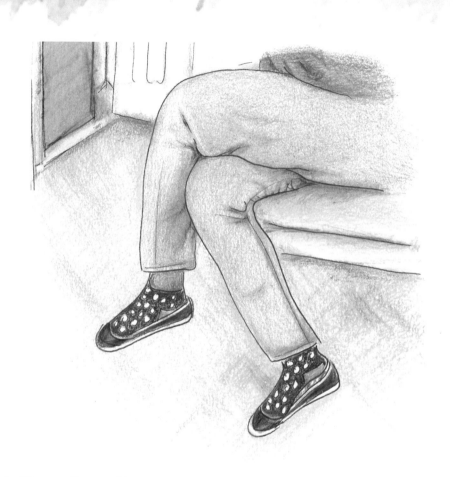

I know! Let's play
sit down.

Chapter 2

"I Like..."

"I like your picture."

E, e

"I like your eyes."
"I like your hat."

R, r

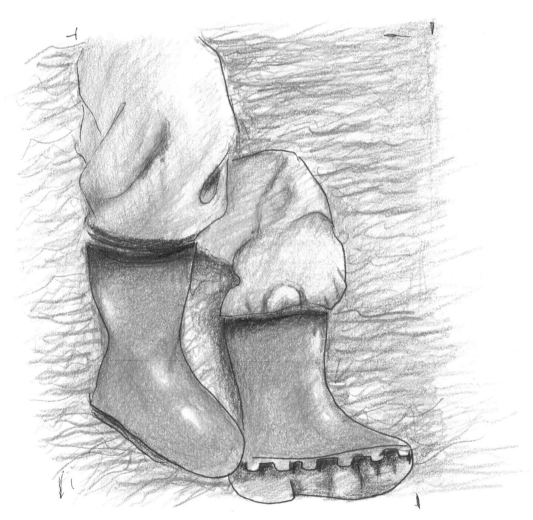

"I like your red boots."

H, h

"I like your hair."

"I like your hair too!"

I, i

"I like you."

Chapter 3

How Beautiful Is That!

X, x

Titled: Rocket Ship

By: Jeo

Titled: Grammy

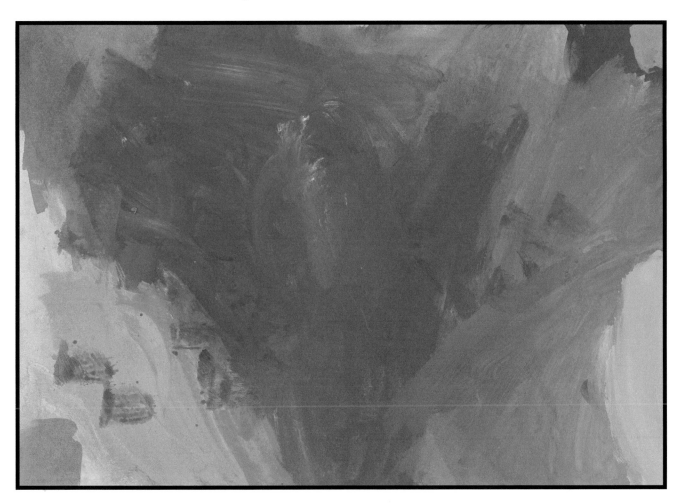

By: Naomi

J, j

Titled: Just Beautiful!

By: Jeo

Titled: Castle

By: Arianna

V, v

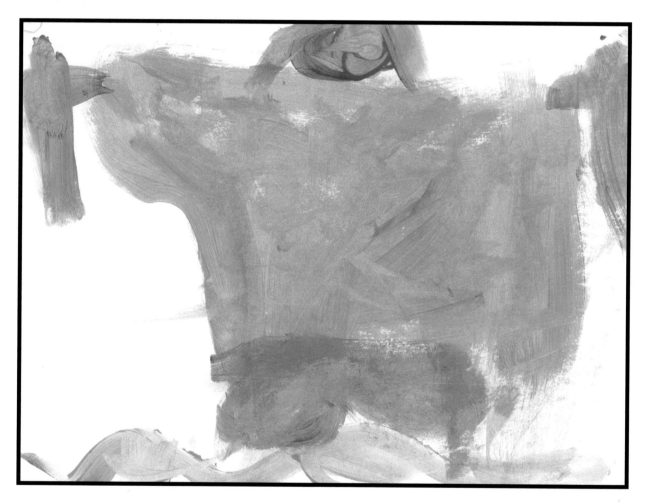

Titled: Valentine's Day

By: Kennedy

K, k

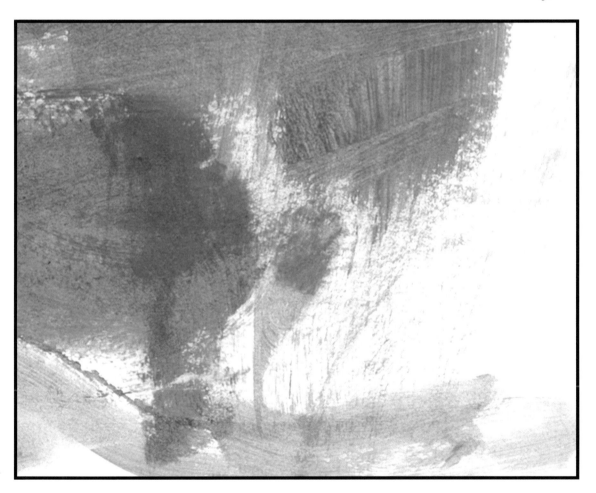

Children keep painting.

Chapter 4

Seasons

W, w

Winter is cold.

F, f

Fall is colorful.

P, p

That's when we celebrate harvest!

Pumpkins galore!

Everything's coming
up clovers!

C, c

G, g

I'm grateful for spring and all that
God has given to us.

Ş, ş

Summer is perfect for outside play...

and we celebrate

Independence Day!

A, a

All four seasons
are quite lovely!

Q, q

Chapter 5

Lummy Nunch

Clean up! Lunch time.

N, n

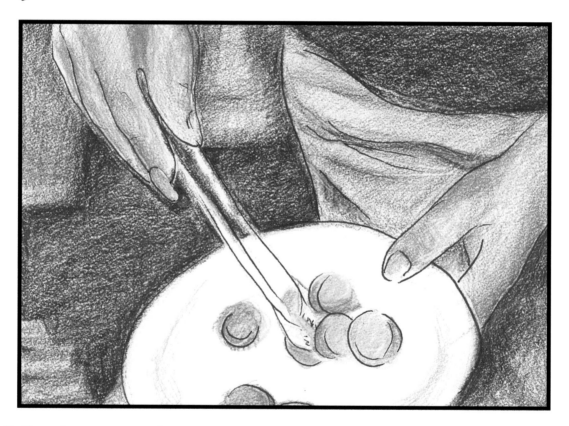

NaNa is serving.

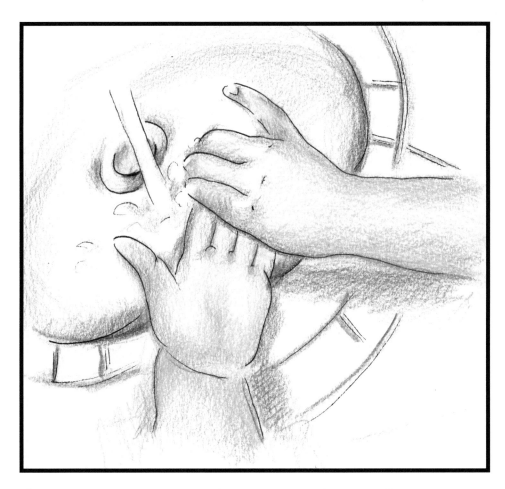

Don't forget to wash your hands.

Y, y

Yummy!

Chomp!

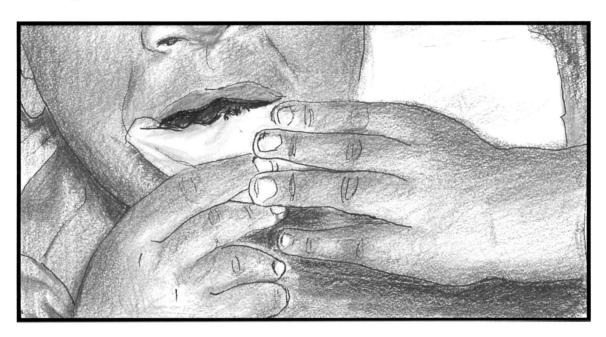

Chomp!

Vitamin C ...

...and vitamin D.

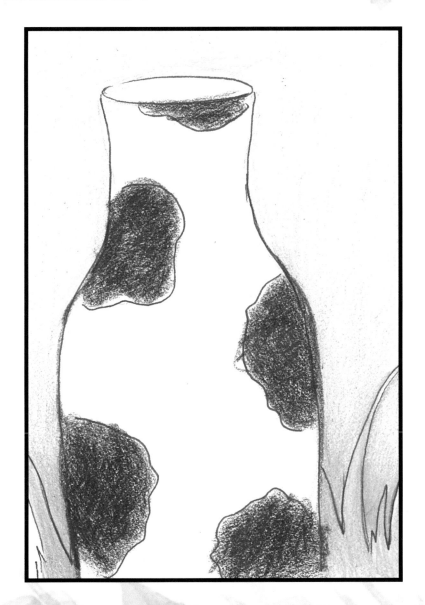

Yummy Lunch!

"Thank you NaNa for the lummy nunch!"

M, m

More please.

Chapter 6

Nap Time!

Z, z

Zzzz…

The End

A B C D

E F G H

I J K L

M N O P

Q R S T

U V W X

Y Z

a b c d e

f g h i j

k l m n o

p q r s t

u v w x y

z

Printed in the United States
By Bookmasters